Finding
Joy

Other Women of Faith Bible Studies

WOMEN OF FAITH℠
BIBLE STUDY SERIES

Finding
Joy

Written by

TRACI MULLINS

ZondervanPublishingHouse
Grand Rapids, Michigan

A Division of HarperCollins*Publishers*

Finding Joy
Copyright © 1998 by Women of Faith, Inc.

Requests for information should be addressed to:

ZondervanPublishingHouse
Grand Rapids, Michigan 49530

ISBN: 0-310-21336-3

General Editor, Traci Mullins
Cover and interior illustration by Jim Dryden
Interior design by Sue Vandenberg Koppenol

Printed in the United States of America

00 01 02 03 04 /❖ EP/ 10 9 8

CONTENTS

FOREWORD

The best advice I ever received was in 1955. I was twenty-three. Somebody had the good sense to say to me, "Luci, if you want to give yourself a gift, learn all you can about the Bible. Start going to a Bible class and don't stop until you have some knowledge under your belt. You won't be sorry." Having just graduated from college, I was living with my parents, and together we drove more than twenty miles to attend that class. We went four nights a week for two years. I've *never* been sorry.

Nothing I've ever done or learned has meant more to me than those classes. Unless I was on my deathbed, I didn't miss. I went faithfully, took notes, absorbed everything like a sponge, asked questions relentlessly, and loved *every* minute! (I probably drove the teacher crazy.)

Today, more than forty years later, this wonderful storehouse of truth is my standard for living, giving, loving, and learning. It is my Rock and Fortress, the pattern for enjoying abundant life on earth, and for all eternity. I know what I believe, and why. I'm open to change on my tastes, personal opinions, even some of my choices. But change my biblical convictions? No way! They're solid and secure, based on God's inerrant, enduring, and unchanging Word. There's nothing like learning God's truth. As he says, it sets you free.

Women of Faith Bible studies are designed to help you deal with everyday problems and issues concerning you. Experienced and wise women who, like the rest of us, want to know God intimately, have written these lessons. They encourage us to dig into the Scriptures, read them carefully, and respond to thought-provoking questions. We're invited to memorize certain verses as sources of support and guidance, to hide his Word in our heads and hearts.

The clever ideas in these studies make me smile. The stories move my spirit. There are valuable suggestions in dealing with others, quotations that cause me to stop and think. The purpose of every activity is to put "some knowledge under your belt" about the Bible and its relevance for life *this very day.*

Give yourself a gift. Grab your Bible, a pencil, notepad, cup of coffee . . . maybe even a friend . . . and get started. I assure you—you'll *never* be sorry.

LUCI SWINDOLL

HOW TO USE THIS GUIDE

Women of Faith Bible studies are designed to take you on a journey toward a more intimate relationship with Christ by bringing you together with your sisters in the faith. We all want to continue to grow in our Christian lives, to please God, to be a vital part of our families, churches, and communities. But too many of us have tried to grow alone. We haven't found enough places where we feel safe to share our heartaches and joys and hopes. We haven't known how to support and be supported by other women in ways that really make a difference. Perhaps we haven't had the tools.

The guide you are about to use will give you the tools you need to explore a fundamental aspect of your walk with God *with* other women who want to grow, too. You'll not only delve into Scripture and consider its relevance to your everyday life, but you'll also get to know other women's questions, struggles, and victories—many similar, some quite different from your own. This guide will give you permission to be yourself, to share honestly, to care for one another's wounds, and laugh together when you take yourselves too seriously.

Each of the six lessons in this guide is divided into six sections. Most you'll discuss as a group; others you'll cover on your own during the week between meetings.

A Moment for Quiet Reflection. The questions in this section are meant to be answered in a few minutes of privacy sometime before you join your group each week. You may already carve out a regular time of personal reflection in your days, so you've experienced the refreshment and insight these times bring to your soul. However, if words like "quiet," "reflection," and "refreshment" have become unfamiliar to you, let this guide get you started with the invaluable practice of setting aside personal time to think, to rest, to pray. Sometimes the answers you write down to the questions in this section will be discussed as a group when you come together; other times they'll just give you something to ponder deep within. Don't neglect this important reflection time each week, and include enough time to read the introduction to the lesson so you'll be familiar with its focus.

Knowing God's Heart. The questions in this section will take you into the Bible, where you and the women in your group can discover God's heart and mind on the subject at hand. You'll do the Bible study together, reading the Scriptures aloud and sharing your understanding of the passage so all of you can learn together what God has to say about your own heart and life, right now. While you don't need to complete the study questions prior to each group session, it will be helpful for you to read through this part of the lesson beforehand so you can begin thinking about your answers. There is a lot to cover in each lesson, so being somewhat familiar with the content before your meetings will save your group time when you actually do your study together.

Friendship Boosters. A big part of why you've come together is to deepen your friendships with other women and to support each other in meaningful ways. The questions and activities in this section are designed to link you together in bonds of friendship, faith, and joy. Whether you are meeting the other women in your group for the first time or are old friends, this section will boost the quality and pleasure in your relationships as well as give you opportunities to support each other in practical ways.

Just for Fun. God's plan for our lives certainly isn't all work and no play! Central to being a woman of faith is cultivating a joyful spirit, a balanced perspective, and an ability to enjoy life because of God's faithfulness and sovereignty. Every week you'll be given an idea or activity that will encourage you to enjoy your journey, laugh, and lighten your load as you travel the path toward wholehearted devotion together.

Praying Together. Nothing is more important than asking God to help you and your friends as you learn how to live out his truths in your lives. Each time you get together you'll want to spend some time talking to him about your individual and mutual concerns.

Making It Real in Your Own Life. You'll respond to these questions or activities on your own after group meetings, but don't consider them just an afterthought. This section is critical because it will help you discover more ways to apply what you've learned and discussed to your own life in the days and weeks ahead. This section will be a key to making God's liberating truths more real to you personally.

In each section, space is provided after each question for you to record your answers, as well as thoughts stimulated by others' answers during group discussion. While you can gain wisdom from completing parts of this guide on your own, you'll miss out on a lot of the power—and the fun!—of making it a group experience.

One woman should be designated as the group facilitator, but she needn't have any training in leading a Bible study or discussion group. The facilitator will just make sure the discussion stays on track, and there are specific notes to help her in the "Leader's Guide" section at the back of this book. Keeping your group size to between four and eight participants is ideal because then it will be possible for everyone to share each week. The length of time you'll need to complete the lessons together will depend largely on how much the participants talk, so the group facilitator will need to monitor the time to keep it under ninety minutes. The facilitator can also speed up or slow down the group time by choosing to skip some discussion questions or concentrate longer on others. If you decide to do this study in a larger group or Sunday school class, split up into smaller groups for discussion. Especially make sure no one gets left out of the process of building friendships and having fun!

Now that you've studied the map, your journey should go smoothly. Celebrate being women of faith as you travel together. *Enjoy!*

INTRODUCTION
Where's the Joy?

One of the best statements about joy I've ever heard was made by Luci Swindoll: "Life is a happy thing, a festival to be enjoyed rather than a drudgery to be endured."

Sounds great, doesn't it? Who wouldn't want to celebrate more and work less? Who wouldn't jump at the chance to experience life as "a happy thing" rather than a never-ending "to do" list? *Do the laundry. Write to your mother. Pick up the kids from soccer practice. Meet those job demands with a smile, cook his favorite meal, hoe the garden, make the boss look good. Oh, and don't forget to spend quality time with God!*

But sometimes enjoying life is easier said than done, isn't it? When the phone is ringing, the kids are tracking mud across your carpet, your coworker doesn't pull her weight, your best friend is snippy, and your husband responds to your furrowed brow with his ever-sensitive "What's wrong with *you?*" finding the joy (much less the humor!) in the situation doesn't come naturally for most of us. Job could have been speaking for many modern women when he said, "I have no peace, no quietness; I have no rest, but only turmoil. . . . What strength do I have, that I should still hope? What prospects, that I should be patient? Do I have the strength of stone? Is my flesh bronze?" (Job 3:26; 6:11–12). Sometimes life is a real pain!

So what was the apostle Paul talking about when he said, "For the kingdom of God is not a matter of eating and drinking, but of righteousness, peace and *joy* in the Holy Spirit" (Rom. 14:17, emphasis added)?

If we're to get beyond the drudging and trudging to celebrating the abundance God promises to those who know him, then we need his perspective on our lives. We must uncover the beliefs and attitudes that keep us from experiencing the abiding joy we can have even in the mundane or frustrating moments of life.

The dictionary defines joy as "a very glad feeling; delight." What exactly do you have to be glad about? How can you feel delight when things aren't going your way? How can you cultivate a spirit of celebration *every day?*

As a Christian woman, if you've ever asked the question, *Where's the joy?* then this guide is for you. Use it to get to know yourself and other women better, and to discover God's secrets to "an inexpressible and glorious joy" (1 Peter 1:8). It really can be yours.

> *You have made known to me the path of life; you will fill me with joy in your presence, with eternal pleasures at your right hand.*
> PSALM 16:11

Joybusters

*I*f we have the Holy Spirit dwelling within us, then one of the results is supposed to be joy (Galatians 5:22). So why don't all of us experience more
of it, more consistently?

Before we can begin to cultivate more joy in our lives, we need to
take a good look at what prevents this precious spiritual fruit from grow-
ing. Many different weeds can choke it. Neglect and inattention can stunt
it. Carelessness can bust it before it has a chance to thrive. A healthy, happy
soul doesn't grow without tender, diligent care.

In this lesson you'll unearth the various rocks and weeds that
threaten your joy, and you'll help each other begin to find your way back to
the Garden.

A cheerful heart is good medicine,
but a crushed spirit dries up the bones.

PROVERBS 17:22

A Moment
for Quiet Reflection

1. How full is your cup: overflowing, empty as a dry riverbed, or something in between? Indicate below how much joy you have been experiencing in your life lately by filling in the cup to the appropriate level.

2. What do you think are the reasons for your current joy or lack of joy? List the first thing(s) that comes to mind.

3. If your cup isn't quite as full as you'd like it to be, think of a time in your life when it was brimming. What was different then—in your circumstances, your habits, and your attitude?

Knowing God's Heart

1. As a group, briefly share your answers to the personal reflection questions above. This will help you start getting to know where each of you is on your journey toward joy.

2. Take turns reading the following Scripture passages and discuss what they imply about the reasons people lose their joy. Try to identify one specific "joybuster" in each passage.

- Numbers 11:4–6

- Exodus 14:9–12

- Psalm 38:1–6

- Lamentations 1:1–6

- Psalm 13:1–2

- Psalm 119:28

- Job 7:1–16

- Matthew 6:34

- Psalm 55:4–5, 12–14

- Habakkuk 1:2–4

3. Which of the ten joybusters above is *most* interfering with your experience of joy today? Why? (If your personal joy-buster isn't reflected in the verses you just read, name your own.) As you listen to each woman share, make note of her primary joybuster.

4. Think about the past few years of your life. Share with the group which joybusters seem to be chronic for you.

5. Brainstorm together some ways you can bust the threats to your joy before they bust you. Have one person keep a list of the ideas you come up with.

6. Reviewing the list, choose one specific thing you will do to combat your current personal joybuster in the week ahead—or whenever it tries to bust down your door again. Share your strategy with the group and write down each woman's strategy next to her joybuster.

7. No matter what your personal joybusters are, you need not be discouraged. What assurances does Psalm 62:5–8 give you as you continue your journey?

> *Life is simply full of curves—sometimes gentle, pleasant, and surprisingly gratifying and sometimes threatening to overwhelm me in their sharpness. The seat belt insuring my survival is that one profound and simple truth: Jesus loves me.*
>
> MARILYN MEBERG

Friendship Boosters

1. Share one thing that brought you joy in the past week. Even the smallest incident or moment of insight is worth sharing a smile over.

2. Take time now to exchange addresses, phone numbers, and/or e-mail addresses. Consider dropping a funny card in the mail or sending an electronic message this week just to say hi. If you're really brave, contact someone you've just met for the first time or don't know very well. Your card or message might just give her a much-needed "joyboost"!

Just for Fun

A great way to cultivate joy and friendship is to have some *fun!* Keep your eyes peeled this week for something funny in a newspaper, book, or your life. When you find it, call another woman in the group and share a laugh. It may sound silly, but you'll be surprised at how good it will make both of you feel!

> *I think God has given women the power to move on in life through the contagion of laughter....*
> *We laugh so we won't scream.*
>
> BARBARA JOHNSON

Praying Together

Referring to your notes of each other's personal joy-busters, pray together now for each woman's specific concerns. Ask God to help each of you use the simple strategy you've chosen to resist whatever threatens your joy.

> *Circumstances are the rulers of the weak;*
> *they are but the instruments of the wise.*
> SAMUEL LOVER

Making It Real
in Your Own Life

1. Between now and your next group meeting, pay attention to the situations and attitudes that threaten your joy. Make note of them as they come up, and start watching for patterns.

2. Think of someone you know who has a lot of joy in his or her life. If possible, call this person and ask what his or her "secrets" are. Be ready to share your findings with the group next week.

Don't Sweat the Small Stuff

F ew things erode the joy in our lives more quickly and surely than fretting about the basic stuff of living. *How am I going to get this memo typed, return all these phone calls, shop for groceries, pick up the boys from baseball practice, help Katie with her math, finish that Bible study, and read the briefs for tomorrow morning's meeting without losing my cool—or my mind?!*

Since life isn't likely to slow down anytime soon, we all need to learn how to hold on to our joy in the midst of the stress and the whirlwind. And the best way to do that is to keep our perspective in order.

Psychiatrist Richard Carlson was on to something when he wrote in his *New York Times* best-seller, *Don't Sweat the Small Stuff,*

> When we are immobilized by little things—when we are irritated, annoyed, and easily bothered—our (over-) reactions not only make us frustrated but actually get in the way of getting what we want. We lose sight of the bigger picture, focus on the negative, and annoy other people who might otherwise help us. In short, we live our lives as if they were one big emergency! We often rush around looking busy, trying to solve problems, but in reality, we are

often compounding them. Because everything seems like such a big deal, we end up spending our lives dealing with one drama after another. After a while, we begin to believe that everything really is a big deal. We fail to recognize that the way we relate to our problems has a lot to do with how quickly and efficiently we solve them.*

Carlson's advice sounds strangely familiar. Could it be that Jesus gave some of the same advice a couple of thousand years ago?

Now that you're more aware of what steals your joy, you can prepare yourself to guard it more effectively. In this lesson you'll take a closer look at the "small stuff" that eats away at your serenity and steals the joy of your salvation. It's time to get things in perspective.

> *Who of you by worrying can add a single hour to his life?*
>
> JESUS CHRIST

*Richard Carlson, Ph.D., *Don't Sweat the Small Stuff . . . and it's all small stuff* (New York: Hyperion, 1997), 1–2.

A Moment
for Quiet Reflection

1. Make yourself a cup of tea and settle in for a few moments
of solitude. Think about the week past and the week ahead,
and quickly list all the people, situations, and activities—
important or trivial—that are on your mind. Review your
list and underline the ones you're "sweating" about. Bring
your list with you to the group meeting.

Knowing God's Heart

1. Read Luke 10:38–42 together. What do you suppose were
some of the specific things that distracted Martha from
spending time with her divine Guest?

2. From that list of distractions, how many could be considered "small stuff"?

3. Describe a time when you felt and behaved like Martha. What were the consequences?

4. Look again at verse 40. What was Martha's *real* problem?

5. What did Mary's behavior reveal about her beliefs and her relationship with Jesus?

6. Discuss some of your specific behaviors in response to your worries that reveal your true beliefs about God. (Don't be self-conscious—everyone is a "Martha" sometimes!)

7. What do you think Jesus meant by telling Martha that "only one thing is needed" and that the results of her sister's choice would "not be taken away from her"?

8. Describe a time when you became caught up in an activity or event that left you feeling empty in the end. In what ways could truths from this passage have changed your experience?

9. If fretting and controlling generally make us and others unhappy, why do you think they are such popular pastimes? Make a list together of the "pros" and "cons" of taking charge of the people and circumstances that are important to you.

10. Which sister, Martha or Mary, do you think had more joy in her life on a regular basis? Why?

11. If you asked someone during the past week what his or her "secrets" to joy are, share with the group what you learned. Are any of your joyful friend's personal secrets reflected in this lesson? If so, which ones?

> *Don't take yourself too seriously. It just makes life all the harder. It'll all come out in the wash anyway, because God's glory eventually will eclipse everything that goes wrong on this earth.*
>
> LUCI SWINDOLL

Friendship Boosters

1. Write down on a small slip of paper one upcoming situation or activity you're feeling anxious about and pass it to the woman on your right. In the week ahead, call the woman who gave you her worry and ask her how she's feeling about it. Encourage her with something you learned in this lesson; in doing so, you'll also help yourself get your own concerns in perspective.

2. Sometimes our anxieties are the result of feeling like we have to handle too many things on our own. Talk together about how you might help each other with specific tasks or concerns that have you sweating. (For example, you might help another woman get her house clean before her weekend guests arrive. Or a woman might help you keep your sense of humor in the midst of a stressful week by calling you each morning with a silly joke or story.) Sharing one another's burdens can make them seem lighter for each of you.

Just for Fun

Play "Time Warp," a game Dr. Richard Carlson made up to help him keep a healthy perspective on what is really important in life. Referring to the "worry" list you made in "A Moment for Quiet Reflection," place an asterisk beside the items that could be categorized as the "small stuff" of life. (Hint: If you'll probably forget all about it in a month, or a year, it qualifies!) Share at least three of these items with the group and enjoy the opportunity to laugh at yourself for blowing some things out of proportion. To fine-tune your perspective even more, share stories of some of the "small" things you recall sweating about and how they worked out. Chances are, you'll enjoy a laugh or two as you compare notes about your perceived emergencies.

Praying Together

Spend a few minutes thanking God for giving us so much wisdom through his Word about how to live our daily lives peacefully and joyfully. One at a time, offer a one-sentence prayer of gratitude for a specific insight you gained from this lesson.

> *So many of us live our lives as if the secret purpose is to somehow get everything done. We stay up late, get up early, avoid having fun, and keep our loved ones waiting.... I find that if I remind myself (frequently) that the purpose of life isn't to get it all done but to enjoy each step along the way and live a life filled with love, it's far easier for me to control my obsession with completing my list of things to do.*
> RICHARD CARLSON, PH.D.

Making It Real
in Your Own Life

1. Read Psalm 27:4–6 and write it out in your own words. Spend a few minutes meditating on it each day this week, considering which of the benefits of keeping your focus on God are real in your life right now.

2. Next time you find yourself running around (literally or figuratively) as if everything in your life is an emergency, STOP. Take a deep breath, count slowly to ten, and come up with some specific ways you can handle things more calmly and efficiently. (It helps to ask God for some ideas!)

> *Once we comprehend the brevity of life here and the importance of eternity with him, everything falls into place. God is in charge of it all.*
> BARBARA JOHNSON

Don't Sweat the Big Stuff Either

Okay, so you can see how you might have blown some of the "small stuff" of life just a wee bit out of proportion. And you're willing to concede that you've spent inordinate amounts of time fretting about things that ultimately came out in the wash. But let's face it: some things in life are BIG. SERIOUS. SCARY. Maybe we can learn to chill out when the dishes don't get done or the dog piddles on the carpet or we have a rough day at the office. But does God really expect us to be joyful in the face of stuff that has more significant ramifications?

Maybe you're going through a painful divorce . . . or looking forward to getting married. Perhaps you're expecting a child . . . or wrestling for the soul of one you've already got. Maybe you're struggling with your health or finances or teenagers, and every corner you turn seems to thrust you into a new battle zone.

Big stuff. Life is full of it.

So what's a woman to do? Pretend it's not as bad as it is? Moan and groan until everyone within griping distance gets sick of you? Gird your loins (do women have those?) and ride into battle? Hightail it and run?

God has a better way. A way that allows us to hold on to our joy no matter what heartbreaks or anxieties or opportunities we face. It's a way that has nothing to do with us and everything to do with him.

If you're facing some big stuff—good or bad—you need not let your fear dictate all your feelings and actions. Your big stuff may indeed be big . . . but God is bigger.

> *In this world you will have trouble. But take heart!*
> *I have overcome the world.*
> JESUS CHRIST

A Moment
for Quiet Reflection

1. What is the "biggest" thing you have ever experienced? List all the emotions you had in response to it.

2. Regardless of how things turned out, what specific evidence can you see of God's faithfulness to you before, during, and after the "big thing" passed. (If you're still in the middle of it, answer as much of the question as you can.)

Knowing God's Heart

1. As the divinely appointed leader of God's chosen people, Moses always had his hands full as he ushered the unruly bunch across deserts and through seas. In Numbers 13, the Israelites approach the "land of milk and honey" God had been promising them since the days of Abraham. Good stuff! At the Lord's command, Moses sends a dozen scouts on ahead to scope out the territory and report back on what they see. Read their account in Numbers 13:26–33. What "big stuff" did they report that got the people sweating?

2. Caleb saw the same big stuff the other scouts saw, yet he brought back a different report. Why do you think he had confidence while most felt hopelessness and terror?

3. Think of a time when you were marching along in your faith, only to be brought up short by an overwhelming or frightening obstacle. Tell the group what that obstacle was and how you initially responded to it. (Can you relate to the scouts' grasshopperish feelings?)

4. Read the details of the masses' response in Numbers 14:1–4. What does it reveal about them and their beliefs?

5. In verse 9, Caleb and Joshua urge the people to hold on to their faith and put aside their fear of the "big stuff" looming in front of them. What reason do these two godly men give for their unwavering confidence?

6. How did the people respond to Caleb's and Joshua's encouragement (verse 10)? Why?

7. Have you ever become angry at someone who rebuked you for your fear or lack of faith? If so, tell the group why you felt that way and how you responded.

8. In verse 11 Moses got an earful from God. What reasons did God give for his anger against the people he loved?

9. The Israelites' fears became self-fulfilling prophecies. According to verses 26–37, what consequences did they experience as a result of their rebellion and lack of faith?

10. Out of the thousands of people God had wanted to usher into the Promised Land, only two of that group, Caleb and Joshua, were eventually allowed in. What does verse 24 imply about what it takes to please the Lord and receive his promises?

11. What do you think was the "bottom-line" sin of the people who were doomed to wander and die in the wilderness?

> *God's will never takes me where his grace*
> *will not sustain me.*
>
> RUTH HUMLECKER

Friendship Boosters

Divide into groups of two or three, depending on the total size of the group. With your partner(s), discuss the following quote by Luci Swindoll:

> Why is it that we limit God? He generally isn't the one who puts the skids on our hopes and dreams. We do it ourselves.
>
> We think, *I'm too old,* or *I'm not good enough,* or *What will people think?* or *I've never done this before,* or *I can't afford it.* So we don't even move off home plate. We simply strike out at bat.

Share recent examples of ways you have limited God by making some of these statements yourselves. Then spend equal time brainstorming about how each of you could "get off home plate" regarding the challenge or opportunity you've deemed "big stuff." Is it really too big for God to handle?

Just for Fun

It's easy to let the joy and fun drain out of our lives when "big stuff" is going on. Sometimes it can seem impossible to see beyond our present difficulty or believe that life will be peaceful again. Fortunately, we can get a little help from our friends. With the one or two women you got to know better during "Friendship Boosters," brainstorm zany activities you could do together to inject some lightheartedness into your lives. Plan a time in the week ahead to carry out one or more of your wild and crazy ideas and commit yourselves to opening your hearts and minds to a fresh perspective.

Praying Together

Come back together as a group and spend a few minutes praying around your "circle." One at a time, say a one-sentence prayer for the woman on your right, asking God to give her a specific blessing that relates to the lesson you've studied together. For example,

- God, give _____ the unwavering faith of Caleb, who knew you were a God of your word.
- Lord, help _____ face her personal giants with courage and confidence because of your protection and might.
- Father, remind _____ that she can choose at any moment of the day to reaffirm her trust in you and change her perspective on her situation.

We may not be able to physically go back and make a new start, but we can start from now and make a brand-new end. We can begin today to choose to see the world afresh, even when hard things are happening.
BARBARA JOHNSON

Making It Real
in Your Own Life

1. Read Psalm 118:6–9. If you're facing "big stuff" in your life right now, what specific encouragement can you draw from the psalmist's confident words?

2. Read the verses aloud, this time replacing the words "man" with whoever or whatever feels threatening to you right now. Continue repeating your "personalized" verses until your voice begins to ring with faith and confidence.

3. Write out Psalm 118:6–14 and try memorizing it in the week ahead. Then any time you face off against the "big stuff" of life, you'll have the "sword of the Spirit" in your back pocket.

> *When you look at challenges as a series of tests,*
> *you begin to see each issue you face as an opportunity*
> *to grow, a chance to roll with the punches....*
> *If, on the other hand, you see each new issue you face*
> *as a serious battle that must be won in order to survive,*
> *you're probably in for a very rocky journey.*
> *The only time you're likely to be happy is when*
> *everything is working out just right. And we all*
> *know how often that happens.*
> RICHARD CARLSON, PH.D.

LESSON FOUR

Get a Grip
on Griping

Do you ever just want to throw back your head and bellow, 'Gimme a break'?" Which one of us could honestly answer Patsy Clairmont's question in anything other than the affirmative? She's right when she says, "Life has a way of mounting up until we are slumping down. Soon our joyful noises turn into grumpy groans."

And who could blame us? I mean life is just so . . . daily! Sometimes it seems we'll never get off the same old merry-go-round: morning comes too early and no day is long enough. Surely we deserve a little more variety, excitement, relaxation, and pampering. After all, the people down the street seem to have it made. Why do they get all the breaks? Who can we call to complain? There should be a 1–800-Whaa-Whaa-Whaa! hotline for us to dial any time, day or night.

Griping comes as naturally as breathing to some of us—certainly more naturally than praising! And it has always been so, down through the centuries. If you're in "gimme a break!" mode, this lesson should help you get a grip so you can get back to joy.

> *The more you complain, the longer God lets you live.*
> BARBARA JOHNSON

A Moment
for Quiet Reflection

1. When was the last time you felt like bellowing for a break? Is the thing that was frustrating you something you find yourself complaining about often?

2. On a scale of one to ten, how "whiny" do you consider yourself to be? (How do you think your spouse or best friend would rate you on the same scale?)

3. What "blessing" do you find it most difficult to be thankful for at times? Your job? Your kids? Your pocketbook? How many times a week would you guess it interferes with your experience of joy?

Knowing God's Heart

1. On the road to Canaan, God's people had one adventure
after another. And they evidently got bored with one of
them. Have someone read Numbers 11:1–20 aloud. What
were the Israelites complaining about now?

2. Why were the people so dissatisfied with God's daily provi-
sion of "bread from heaven"?

3. In verse 5, the people exposed a pretty crazy quirk in their
thinking. What was it?

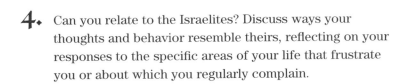

4. Can you relate to the Israelites? Discuss ways your thoughts and behavior resemble theirs, reflecting on your responses to the specific areas of your life that frustrate you or about which you regularly complain.

5. How do you suppose God feels about your whining? Why?

6. One at a time, try filling in the blank in this sentence: If only _____, I would be content.

7. How much stock do you put in this belief, now that you've stated it clearly? Do you think it is valid? (Be honest!) Why or why not?

8. Why was God so angry with his people when they demanded meat instead of manna?

9. Have you ever given a gift to someone who seemed ungrateful, or who complained about it outright? (Children can be especially good at this!) How did it make you feel?

10. How do you feel about the way God responded to his people (verses 19–20)? Why?

11. What do you think was the Israelites' most serious offense? Discuss the reasons for your opinion.

12. Have you ever had your prayers answered, only to wish you could take them back? If so, you have something else in common with God's original chosen ones! Share your experience with the group.

Friendship Boosters

1. Divide into groups of two or three—choose different women than you talked with during the last session. Share one thing in your life that you wish was different than it is. Explain why.

2. Now practice turning your gripes into praises by changing your focus from what you want to what you have. For example, instead of wishing your husband was more attentive or empathetic (and criticizing him for his shortcomings), be grateful if he's gentle or fun-loving. Instead of wishing you'd gotten that raise you deserve, be grateful if you have enough money to pay this month's electric bill. Help each other come up with different ways to look at the things that cause you to grumble. During the week ahead, call each other and compare notes on how this exercise affects your daily perspective.

> *We discover that we receive guidance for our lives to just about the extent that we stop making demands upon God to give it to us on order and on our terms.*
> ALCOHOLICS ANONYMOUS

Just for Fun

Barbara Johnson offers some wise advice for combating the fear and self-pity that often go along with the "big stuff" of life: "The next time you're feeling down," she says, "think about all the terrible things that didn't happen to you." Divide your group into two "teams" and take her prescription for joy by calling out your "non-disasters" as quickly as they come to mind. (Appoint a leader for each team who will keep score by counting the number of ideas shouted out by your team's players.) In any group of women there will be some who have experienced a truly terrible thing or two. Be sensitive to this, but let some silliness prevail as you come up with your list. After all, you didn't get paint splashed onto your mink coat. Did you?

Praying Together

One at a time, complete this sentence in as many ways as you can: "Lord, thank you for . . ." Spend several minutes offering these simple prayers of gratitude to God. When you close your prayer time, say together the following prayer by A. Philip Parham: "Give us, O Lord, steadfast hearts, which no unworthy thoughts can drag down; unconquered hearts, which no tribulation can wear out; upright hearts, which no unworthy purpose may tempt aside. Amen."

> *Our circumstances may be dreadful and riddled with reasons for discouragement or sorrow, but that doesn't mean those moments are utterly devoid of happiness.*
> LUCI SWINDOLL

Making It Real
in Your Own Life

1. Begin each day this week with a prayer of gratitude. No matter what is going on in your life, find something to thank God for and make expressing your gratitude your morning habit. Record your praises in a blank journal that you designate as your "gratitude book."

2. Before you go to sleep each night, add at least one more thing to your gratitude book. Notice the ways in which "book-ending" your days with praise helps shift your perspective and increases your joy.

> *So much of the joy in life depends on how we see things. . . . It seems that, regardless of our circumstances, joy comes to those who look for it.*
> BARBARA JOHNSON

Remember
When ...

Have you ever heard the phrase "compare and despair"? That's what the Israelites did repeatedly as God led them by Moses through the desert. Every time they found their current circumstances wanting, they recalled the "good old days" when they were slaves in Egypt! The comparison always led them to obnoxious wailing and fearful despair. If their defective memory hadn't had such grave implications, their behavior would be almost comical.

The reason we're tempted to laugh, however, isn't because we find their behavior incomprehensible, is it? It's because we can so easily identify with their all-too-human twist in perspective. When things aren't going our way, our first inclination is to wail (there's a part of each of us that never made it beyond the crib!). And the main reason for that is because our memory is so short. We can easily remember the disappointment of this morning, but when it comes to recalling the mercies God showed us last month, forget it!

The psalmists had keen insight into this foible of ours. That's why they gave so much press to the power of recalling the days of old—not so we can moan and groan about what we think we've lost, but so we can rejoice in the undeniable record of God's faithfulness to his faithless people.

When our frame of reference is out of kilter, "remembering when" can lead quickly to the despair God's fickle children experienced. But when we look back on the past in context, remembering can be one of the most effectual tools we can use to restore our confidence in the God who never leaves or forsakes us. And that's reason for rejoicing!

> *Our limited perspective, our hopes and fears become our measure of life, and when circumstances don't fit our ideas, they become our difficulties.*
> BENJAMIN FRANKLIN

A Moment
for Quiet Reflection

1. When was the last time you "compared and despaired"?
Write down all the feelings you experienced as a result.

2. Did any specific actions result from this approach to your
problem? If so, what were they?

3. Now "relive" the episode in your mind, replacing your
despairing thoughts and behavior with those that focus
on God and his goodness and faithfulness. How might
your experience have been different if you'd tried this in
the first place?

Knowing God's Heart

1. Ask a couple of women to volunteer to share their answers to the reflection questions above. Keep their experience (and yours) in mind as you begin your study of the Word.

2. Read Psalm 78:40–43 together. What is the primary reason Asaph gives for the Israelites' rebellion?

3. If only God's people had thought to use the tool the author of Psalm 42 wields so effectively. According to verses 5–6, what is this tool?

4. Now take a look at Psalm 63:1–7, where David's behavior during his own desert experience stands in stark contrast to the Israelites' before him. Discuss at least four key differences.

5. In Psalm 143, David teaches us more about how to deal with distress in a productive rather than rebellious or destructive way. Identify at least five lessons from this prayer that any believer can apply in her own life.

6. Of all the lessons Psalms 63 and 143 teach, which one is the hardest for you to apply when you're in distress? Why?

7. Recall a time when you did use one of these tools. What were the results? Encourage each other with your experiences.

8. Identify one thing in your life right now that scares or upsets you, and share it with the group. (It can be small stuff, big stuff, bad stuff, good stuff.)

9. Now go back around the circle and discuss which of the lessons David exemplifies that you'd like to learn to apply to your situation. Give your reasons and how you think the new approach might alter your feelings or circumstances.

> *Don't let the beaten path you travel daily beat you down.... Leave your baggage of fear, regret, guilt, and disappointment behind you and say, "I'm outta here. I'm going to try another way of getting to joy."*
>
> LUCI SWINDOLL

Friendship Boosters

Pair up with the woman whose birthday is closest to yours (day and month, not year!). Tell each other one story of God's faithfulness to you in the past. Keep pertinent notes while the other is speaking. Sometime in the weeks or months ahead, write your friend a "letter from God," recounting what he did for her (i.e., "Dear _____, Remember when I encouraged you during that difficult time with your daughter? You need never despair because I will always come through for you.") Include as many details of the woman's story as you can remember. Mail her the letter sometime when you know she's discouraged or least expects to hear from God.

Just for Fun

Remember the "memory" game you used to play at parties when you were a child? One girl would start by making a statement like, "My name is Kim and I have a dog named Peanut." Then the next girl would repeat Kim's statement and add her own: "My name is Jill, Kim has a dog named Peanut, and I have a brother named Mark." Then Mary would add, "My name is Mary, Kim has a dog named Peanut, Jill has a brother named Mark, and I have a cat named Mercedes." You get the picture.

Play the memory game with your group, recalling the best gifts you've ever received: "My name is Jennifer and the best gift I ever received was a shiny new bike." "My name is Susan, the best gift Jennifer ever received was a shiny new bike, and the best gift I received was an emerald ring." By the time you get around the circle, you'll probably be in stitches—not to mention embarrassed that you can't remember every gift you've each received. The Israelites' short memory about God's blessings isn't so hard to understand!

Praying Together

Following David's example, pray for each other's concerns in a productive and faith-affirming way. Affirm the truths that David did as you bring each other to God ("Lord, even though some things look bleak right now to _____, we know you are a God of power and mercy.") Remember that God does not ask us to deny our feelings (even when they're gripe-laden); but he does want us to bring them to *him*, not just to each other. He is the one who has the wisdom to counsel and the power to transform.

> *When we think that God cannot or will not help us,*
> *we leave ourselves wide open to fearsome results.*
> *However, when we are convinced that God's power*
> *is greater than any evil that could befall us, we*
> *can live with confidence and hope.*
>
> A. PHILIP PARHAM

Making It Real
in Your Own Life

1. Psalms 105 and 106 are wonderful accounts of a faithful
God's love for a faithless people. Take time to read them
slowly and meditatively, making note of the events and
truths that particularly encourage you in your own journey
of faith.

2. Now write your own "psalm of remembrance." Pray that
God will help you remember his specific acts of faithfulness to you, and then record them in a poem of praise.

I will remember the deeds of the LORD;
yes, I will remember your miracles of long ago.
I will meditate on all your works
and consider all your mighty deeds.
Your ways, O God, are holy.
What god is so great as our God?
PSALM 77:11–13

Joyboosters

As Christians, the ultimate boost to our joy is summed up by Jesus' words to his disciples shortly before he left them to ascend to his Father: "Now is your time of grief, but I will see you again and you will rejoice, and no one will take away your joy" (John 16:22). Jesus comforted his friends with these words as he prepared for death, and he fulfilled them when he appeared to several loved ones after his resurrection.

No matter what we go through on earth, our ultimate joy is guaranteed on the day we see Christ face-to-face. And that day itself is guaranteed if we know him as our personal Savior and Lord. When we leave this world, we will join him—unless he comes back to get us before we've lived out our days (Matt. 24:30–31, 42). Either way, we're in for an eternal joyfest!

Meanwhile . . . we need all the help we can get to live joyfully in a world that regularly rains on our parade. By now you ought to have a good idea of what spoils the spiritual fruit of joy before it has a chance to thrive in your life. You've gained some tools to uproot the weeds and excavate the rocks that threaten to choke your joy. In this lesson you'll continue to fill your tool chest so you are fully equipped to conquer any joybuster that arises from within or without.

> *Life can be a blessing or a curse, problem or*
> *opportunity. It all depends on what we habitually*
> *look for: the good or the bad, God or no God at all.*
> *We can always choose the way of the psalmist who said,*
> *"I believe that I shall see the goodness of the LORD*
> *in the land of the living!"*
>
> A. PHILIP PARHAM

A Moment
for Quiet Reflection

1. Take another stab at the first question posed in this book. How full is your cup: overflowing, empty as a dry riverbed, or something in between? Again, indicate below how much joy you have in your life today.

2. Is your cup more full or less since you began this study? What do you think are the reasons for your answer?

3. What brings you joy? Write down as many "joyboosters" as you can think of in three minutes.

4. Which one gives you the greatest boost today? Why?

Knowing God's Heart

1. As a group, briefly share your answers to the last two questions in "A Moment for Quiet Reflection." Have someone keep a "master list" of all the joyboosters you've come up with individually.

2. Now take turns reading the following Scripture passages to discover some of the joyboosters the Bible identifies. Look for the specific joybooster described in each passage.

- 1 Thessalonians 5:18

- Psalm 27:10

- Psalm 10:17–18

- Nehemiah 9:17

- Joel 2:23–26

- Lamentations 3:19–24

- Psalm 147:3

- Isaiah 40:27–31

- Luke 12:29–32

- Matthew 13:40–43

3. Which of the ten joyboosters above were on your own list? The group's master list?

4. Of all the truths you just read about in Scripture, are there any whose joy-boosting potential you hadn't considered before? If so, which one(s)?

5. This joybooster study certainly isn't exhaustive; Scripture is full of joy-boosting truths and suggestions, and no doubt you have your own "secret recipes" for pulling yourself out of the doldrums. Brainstorm to come up with at least five more joy-boosting tools.

6. Referring to the joybusters you identified in the "Knowing God's Heart" section of Lesson 1 and the first ten joyboosters you discovered above, match up the Scripture references that describe the problem with those that suggest a solution. Work together to connect complementary Scriptures in the "matching game" below:

Joybusters	**Joyboosters**
a. Numbers 11:4–6	a. Psalm 147:3
b. Exodus 14:9–12	b. Luke 12:29–32
c. Psalm 38:1–6	c. 1 Thessalonians 5:18
d. Lamentations 1:1–6	d. Psalm 10:17–18
e. Psalm 13:1–2	e. Lamentations 3:19–24
f. Psalm 119:28	f. Isaiah 40:27–31
g. Job 7:1–16	g. Nehemiah 9:17
h. Matthew 6:34	h. Matthew 13:40–43
i. Psalm 55:4–5, 12–14	i. Joel 2:23–26
j. Habakkuk 1:2–4	j. Psalm 27:10

7. Recall your primary personal joybuster from Lesson 1. (Or pick a new one if it's changed!) Designate one of the joyboosters you've identified as your personal "joy-preserver" in the days or weeks ahead. Discuss why you chose it and how you hope it will keep you afloat in your particular joy-busting situation.

> *How is it that our perspective changes after a moment or two of laughter? Does laughing shake loose the cobwebs that clutch the grim realities? All we know for certain is that nothing appears quite the same after we've loosened our hold on life's dark explanations. Laughter refreshes us.*
>
> KAREN CASEY

Friendship Boosters

1. If you have nagging doubts about whether the truths you've explored in this lesson relate to the realities of your own life in ways that can make a difference, share these doubts with the group. Don't pretend to have more joy than you do, or to understand how to apply things you don't. If you're struggling with something, let your friends know so they can pray for you and share their own experiences in ways that can encourage you.

If instead of doubts or questions you are left with a startling new insight that you believe will increase your joy in the future, share that with the group as well. Rejoice with and support each other wherever you are on your spiritual journey.

2. Write down on a small slip of paper the personal joy-preserver you chose in response to question 7 in "Knowing God's Heart." Write your name and phone number at the top. Put the papers in a "hat" and pass it around so each woman can pick out someone else's joybooster. Commit to keeping in touch with the woman whose joybooster you've chosen. Call her during the weeks ahead to ask her how she's doing and how the lessons she learned during this study are affecting her life. As an act of gratitude for the measure of joy God has given you, be your friend's faithful "joy-buddy" on the journey ahead.

Just for Fun

Remember how you used to make fancy greeting cards and signs and banners when you were a kid? At one time or another most of us have gotten ourselves covered with paste and glitter and felt-tip ink in the pursuit of making something to cheer someone we loved. Well, roll up your sleeves together, put on some fun music, and use your imagination to turn your joy-buddy's joybooster into a "work of art." (And remember, it's the thought that counts!) Present it to her with a hug, and enjoy taking home a creation made by the woman who chose *your* personal joy-booster. Put it in a prominent place at home and let it encourage you on your journey.

Praying Together

Join hearts and voices as you offer this prayer of joyful thanksgiving from Psalm 16:5–11:

LORD, you have assigned me my portion and my cup;
you have made my lot secure.
The boundary lines have fallen for me in
*   pleasant places;*
surely I have a delightful inheritance.
I will praise the LORD, who counsels me;
even at night my heart instructs me.
I have set the LORD always before me.
Because he is at my right hand,
I will not be shaken.
Therefore my heart is glad and my tongue rejoices;
my body also will rest secure,
because you will not abandon me to the grave,
nor will you let your Holy One see decay.
You have made known to me the path of life;
you will fill me with joy in your presence,
with eternal pleasures at your right hand.

Follow your prayer with a few moments of silence, thanking God for each woman present and how she has contributed to your joyful journey. Your group leader will close with a final amen.

The journey for most of us is a long one, but we can support each other along the way. We are not isolated. We are all on the same trip; some are simply farther down the road. And we will all arrive to be claimed by the Lord as part of his family. No unclaimed freight in this bunch!

BARBARA JOHNSON

Making It Real
in Your Own Life

In the gratitude book you started (and hopefully are continuing to fill!) in Lesson 4, write out the Scripture verses that correspond to each of the joyboosters you discovered in this lesson. As you read the Word in the weeks and months ahead, add other joyboosters you find suggested in Scripture. Now your gratitude book has become your joy book! Keep it with your Bible and write in it regularly. It will become for you a permanent source of encouragement that can boost your joy for years to come.

> *Rejoice in the Lord always. I will say it again: Rejoice!*
> PHILIPPIANS 4:4

LEADER'S GUIDE

LESSON ONE

2. Divide the ten Scripture references among the women and give them a few moments to look up the passages. Then have each woman read her verses aloud, pausing between each passage for discussion.

The kinds of circumstances and attitudes that eclipsed the joy of God's children centuries ago still do so today.

- Numbers 11:4–6—focusing on what we don't have: discontent, self-pity
- Exodus 14:9–12—fear that God isn't big enough for our problems: despair
- Psalm 38:1–6—sin and guilt
- Lamentations 1:1–6—loss of personal strength and prestige
- Psalm 13:1–2—feeling oppressed and abandoned by God
- Psalm 119:28—sorrow, grief, depression
- Job 7:1–16—weariness, futility
- Matthew 6:34—worry
- Psalm 55:4–5, 12–14—betrayal, broken relationships
- Habakkuk 1:2–4—resentment about apparent injustice and God's tolerance of evil

5. A few ideas to stimulate discussion: meditate on God's faithfulness; pray instead of fret; call a friend and share the burden; focus on someone else's needs; do something fun; share a laugh; practice an attitude of gratitude. This is just a beginning!

LESSON TWO

4. Sometimes when God doesn't appear to be actively dealing with the things we've placed high on our "worry" list, we conclude that he simply doesn't care about what most concerns us. It's easy to feel "worried and upset" when we believe we're alone in our struggles, and our frustration can turn to anger toward God for appearing so "callous." See Mark 4:35–38 for another example of Jesus' friends and their bewilderment about Jesus' "blasé" attitude.

5. It's easy to *say* we believe God loves us and cares about our problems, but our actions reveal our true beliefs. If, like Martha, we're unable to curb the driven and anxious behaviors we depend on to "get things taken care of," we may believe that God can't be trusted to tend to what we feel is important in our lives. If, on the other hand, we're able to rest in

his presence, like Mary did, our behavior will be less controlling and frantic. Mary loved being close to Jesus more than anything else, and she clearly believed that whatever he had to say deserved her undivided attention and would bring her great reward.

7. Jesus was not implying that no work ever needed to be done or that busy, productive people ought to be ashamed of themselves. However, he was stressing kingdom values—so different from the world's—that call his followers to keep daily tasks in perspective. No activity is more important than spending quality time with him, and cultivating a relationship with him is the only activity that will substantially enrich the human soul.

Friendship Boosters. Have small slips of paper and pens on hand.

LESSON THREE

1. The land God had promised to his people was fraught with dangers. Not only were the cities large and well guarded, but they were inhabited by all the Israelites' worst enemies. Among these enemies were the Amalekites, a fierce tribe that killed for pleasure and gained power by raiding and taking over land belonging to others; the Amorites and Canaanites, idol-worshiping pagans whose greatest pleasures came from their wine and women; and the Anakites, literally "big" bullies who towered seven to nine feet tall. No wonder the majority of God's people were terrified!

2. From all appearances, it seemed that God's people were done for if they dared go forward into the Promised Land. Verse 30 implies that Caleb was able to see beyond appearances because he believed that God would fulfill his long-standing promise to his people: the land was theirs for the taking because it had been chosen by God for his chosen ones.

4. The people's response to God might be summed up as "Thanks for nothing!" After spending years as slaves in Egypt and making an arduous journey across the desert to supposed freedom and prosperity, the obstacles in the Promised Land seemed to be some kind of cosmic joke at their expense! They instantly succumbed to anger, bitterness, doubt, and despair, believing that God could not be trusted to bring them safely into the land he'd promised them. They even seemed to assume that God would almost gladly let the weakest and most precious among them, their wives and children, be taken as plunder. Within seconds they were ready to backtrack all the way to the country that had held them and their ancestors captive for centuries. If the group has time, look at a parallel account of this scene in Deuteronomy 1:21–28. Here the people go so far as to accuse God of "hating" them (talk about paranoid!), and they blame the scouts for their faithlessness ("Our brothers have *made* us lose heart").

5. Caleb and Joshua had absolute confidence in the protective power of God's presence. They trusted that he would be faithful to his promise and that victory would belong not to the strongest people, but to those most favored by God. In spite of what they saw with their eyes, these men didn't waver in their faith that God could clobber the biggest bullies the land could dish up.

6. Rather than invigorate and empower the people, Caleb's and Joshua's confidence had the opposite effect. The whole assembly responded with murderous thoughts. These two fanatics needed to be taken out! Perhaps the people responded this way out of guilt-ridden anxiety; the men's faith in the face of overwhelming odds stood out in bold relief to their own contempt for God's plan, and killing the "voice of conscience" might have seemed the easiest way to silence the condemnation they were bringing on themselves. Or perhaps they just thought these two were nuts who had taken their religious zeal too far. If the assembly didn't deal with them swiftly, the men might actually convince everyone to march forward to certain death.

8. God was clearly dismayed at how impossible it was to convince his people of his power and faithfulness. From generation to generation, he had performed countless miracles and given the people obvious signs of his presence and devotion to them, yet they still refused to believe in him. He took this very personally! In fact, he felt like an object of his people's contempt instead of their love.

10. God has many blessings in store for us, just as he did for his people in Moses' time. But we can miss out on the "Promised Land" in our own lives if we refuse to trust the path he has chosen for us. Caleb's "different spirit" seems to be summed up by the faith-full beliefs he enthusiastically proclaims as well as his willingness to follow the Lord with single-minded and wholehearted devotion, in spite of the appearance of impending disaster.

11. The fact that God's people were afraid of the giants in the Promised Land was probably not what concerned God most; he has instilled in us a natural evasive response to danger. God might not have been most dismayed by the fact that the people's first response to the scouts' bad report was weeping and terror and "creative problem solving" ("We should choose a leader and go back to Egypt"). What appears to have most aggrieved God was the people's personal contempt for him: rather than trusting in the love that had never failed them, they accused God of being their enemy. The bottom line of all their complaints was their self-reliance: instead of relying on God's wisdom and might, they looked to their own resources for survival. When God's people forget or refuse to put their hope in God alone, they ultimately panic.

LESSON FOUR

2. Aside from the obvious (their boredom with the monotonous diet), the people's discontent grew from comparing their current diet with the one they recalled enjoying in the past. When we compare, we have a natural tendency to romanticize whatever we don't have and exaggerate the negatives of what we do have.

3. The same people who had lived in oppression and slavery at the mercy of their enemies, the Egyptians, are now remembering their captivity almost fondly! They are actually pining away for "the good old days" when they could eat all the garlic and onions they wanted (yum!). They recall the food being "without cost," but conveniently forget its enormous price tag. The implication is clear that they think they'd be better off if they'd stayed put in the land from which God had mercifully liberated them.

8. The manna was a clear sign of God's faithfulness to his people. He expected them to receive each day's fresh supply as the gracious gift that it was and to use it to build not only their physical strength but also their faith in his character. Instead, they insisted that they knew better what would satisfy them—and this heavenly pablum certainly wasn't it! Their response was essentially "Thanks, but no thanks," and their ingratitude and arrogance angered the Lord.

10. To the woman unfamiliar with the entire history of God's dealing with his chosen ones, his response might seem a bit unfair or extreme. After all, the Israelites had been eating the same thing every day for what seemed like an eternity, and all they wanted was a bit of variety to spice up the menu! But when understood in context, God's decision to practically gag them with the object of their desire is more than just. Year after year he had proved his faithfulness to his people, yet nothing he ever did silenced their perpetual grumbling.

11. The Israelites' whining and wailing offended God because it reflected their ingratitude and lack of faith. Their pining away for Egypt was certainly offensive because it implied that God didn't know what he was doing when he led them into the desert and couldn't be trusted to meet their needs, even though he had been doing so faithfully for years. But verse 20 indicates that their greatest offense was their personal rejection of God. Even though he demonstrated his loving presence day after day, his people did not love him in return.

LESSON FIVE

2. God's people grieved, vexed, tested, and rebelled against him for one reason: "They did not remember his power." The record shows that whenever their abominably short memory was jogged (usually through

great catastrophe), they repented and returned to him—but it was never long before they repeated the absurd cycle.

3. The tool is memory and its power is affirmed in verse 6. When despair comes knocking and all seems lost, it's time to reach for the tool. "My soul is downcast . . . *therefore* I will remember you."

4. David's approach could not be more different from the desert wanderers'. First, in his desperate need, the first words out of his mouth are not complaints; they are affirmations of his personal, passionate relationship with God and his commitment to seeking him in the midst of distress. Second, his desire to seek and honor God leads immediately to a restored memory: he easily recalls witnessing God's power and glory in the past. Third, recalling God's character and might prompts a confident affirmation of faith: "Your love is better than life," which results in copious praise. Finally, David commits to holding tight to his memories during the "night" so that he can rest and rejoice under God's protection.

5. First, David does not pretend that things are better than they are; he pours out his genuine distress to one he believes cares about him. His honest lament doesn't reek of self-pity or anger at God. Second, he prays with a humble spirit. Unlike the Israelites who demanded things of God because of their "entitlement" as his people, David acknowledges that no one is righteous or deserves God's mercy. Third, he gives considerable credence to God's actions in the past; he "remembers," "meditates," and "considers" *everything* God has done for humankind. This focus on God's goodness and faithfulness fuels his pursuit of God as the only one who can help him. (No "I think I'll go back to Egypt" here!) Fourth, he makes it clear that being rescued is not his only goal; he longs just as passionately to know and do God's will in his life. Finally, his request for salvation isn't for his own sake, but for God's glory. He prays as a servant to his Master, repeatedly affirming God's good character and his own humble dependence.

LESSON SIX

2. Divide the ten Scripture references among the women and give them a few moments to look up the passages. Then have each woman read her verses aloud, pausing between each passage for discussion.

The truths and actions that buoyed God's people during Bible times can still boost our joy today.

- 1 Thessalonians 5:18—Giving thanks and cultivating an attitude of gratitude will always boost our joy.
- Psalm 27:10—Even if the most important people in our lives reject us, God will not.
- Psalm 10:17–18—God can be trusted to hear us in our distress and defend us with his might.

- Nehemiah 9:17—No matter how gravely we sin, God in his love offers us grace and compassion.
- Joel 2:23–26—God is a God of restoration. When we are brought low through loss and defeat, God can be trusted to renew and exalt us once again.
- Lamentations 3:19–24—When we go through times of testing or discipline and feel that God is very far away, we can draw encouragement and hope from the fact that we will experience the joy of his presence if we wait for him. He is a loving and faithful God who is true to his word, and his compassion never fails.
- Psalm 147:3—God specializes in healing broken hearts and treating emotional wounds.
- Isaiah 40:27–31—During times of weariness and discouragement, we can anticipate with confidence that God will renew our strength and increase our power in his time.
- Luke 12:29–32—The Lord understands our basic needs and is intimately concerned about them. His Shepherd-heart can be trusted to give us tender care, so we need not fret about our well-being.
- Matthew 13:40–43—The Lord will eventually judge the earth once and for all, meting out justice and vengeance as his wisdom dictates. Justice is not our concern, it is his, and we can have complete confidence that righteousness will prevail.

6. Answers to matching game:

Joybusters	Joyboosters
a	c
b	j
c	d
d	g
e	i
f	e
g	a
h	f
i	b
j	h

Friendship Boosters. Have small slips of paper and pens on hand, as well as a "hat."

Just for Fun. Gather art supplies you have on hand, and/or call some of the other women and ask them to bring various supplies to the group this week. Be sure to include colorful construction paper, scissors, glue, crayons and markers, bright stickers, and any "paste-on" items you can think of. And don't forget the glitter!

FAITH

Women of Faith Bible studies are based on the popular
Women of Faith conferences.

Women of Faith is partnering with Zondervan Publishing House,
Integrity Music, *Today's Christian Woman* magazine, and Campus Crusade
to offer conferences, publications, worship music, and inspirational gifts
that support and encourage today's Christian women.

Since their beginning in January of 1996, the Women of Faith conferences
have enjoyed an enthusiastic welcome by women across the country.

Call 1-888-49-FAITH for the many conference locations and dates available.

www.women-of-faith.com

**See the following page for additional information
about Women of Faith products.**

Look for these faith-building resources from Women of Faith:

Friends Through Thick & Thin by Gloria Gaither, Peggy Benson,
    Sue Buchanan, and Joy Mackenzie
        Hardcover 0-310-21726-1

We Brake for Joy! by Patsy Clairmont, Barbara Johnson, Marilyn Meberg,
    Luci Swindoll, Sheila Walsh, and Thelma Wells
        Hardcover 0-310-22042-4

Bring Back the Joy by Sheila Walsh
        Hardcover 0-310-22023-8
        Audio Pages 0-310-22222-2

The Joyful Journey by Patsy Clairmont, Barbara Johnson,
    Marilyn Meberg, and Luci Swindoll
        Softcover 0-310-22155-2
        Audio Pages 0-310-21454-8

Joy Breaks by Patsy Clairmont, Barbara Johnson,
    Marilyn Meberg, and Luci Swindoll
        Hardcover 0-310-21345-2

Women of Faith Journal
        Journal 0-310-97634-0

Promises of Joy for Women of Faith
        Gift Book 0-310-97389-9

Words of Wisdom for a Woman of Faith
        Gift Book 0-310-97390-2

Prayers for a Woman of Faith
        Gift Book 0-310-97336-8

We want to hear from you. Please send your comments about this book
to us in care of the address below. Thank you.

ZondervanPublishingHouse
Grand Rapids, Michigan 49530
http://www.zondervan.com